Pray Now

2006

Pray Now
2006

Daily Devotions for the Year 2006

Published on behalf of the

OFFICE FOR WORSHIP AND DOCTRINE
OF THE CHURCH OF SCOTLAND

SAINT ANDREW PRESS
EDINBURGH

First published in 2005 by
SAINT ANDREW PRESS
121 George Street, Edinburgh EH2 4YN

Copyright © Office for Worship and Doctrine of the Church of Scotland, 2005

ISBN 0 86153 368 2

British Library Cataloguing in Publication Data
A catalogue record for this book is available from the British Library

Typeset by Waverley Typesetters, Little Walsingham
Printed and bound in Great Britain by Mackay & Inglis Ltd, Glasgow

Contents

Preface

At a simple human level, belonging to the Church is to be part of a group of people who support, challenge, enrich, encourage and sometimes irritate one another. For most of us, the basic unit of our Christian belonging is our local congregation and/or our own family circle. In his rich little book, *Life Together*, the German thinker and martyr Dietrich Bonhoeffer reflects on how easy it is to take the gift of sharing our Christian lives with others for granted. To share our lives with others is indeed a great gift; in many ways it is our life with others which makes us who we are.

When we become part of the Christian community, what a vista opens up before us. We join a community which is not simply bound by our immediate sisters and brothers in congregation and family; we are invited into a fellowship which is world-wide and ages long. We are bound in solidarity with our brothers and sisters across the world and are challenged and inspired by the whole Communion of Saints.

This year's *Pray Now* invites us into this wider company. It gives us tools for prayer and reflection based on the very different groups we encounter in the Bible's pages, groups which all have a contemporary reference and relevance for us today. The groups are not all composed of saints; there are plenty of sinners with cautionary warnings for us also. As we read of the different ways in which this rich collection of humanity encounters God and shares in the life of the world, we will find much to feed our reflection and our prayers.

Pray Now 2006 is commended warmly as a gift to the Church and to each of us in our life of prayer.

LEITH FISHER
Convener of the Panel on Worship until May 2005

Introduction

Having last year explored community from the perspective of 'gifts', the Prayer and Devotion Committee found much to think about, pray about and write about when looking at the various groupings and crowds in the pages of the Old and New Testaments. Many of these groups have parallels in our world today, and we recognise them by their rituals, by how they express their belonging and by the way they share experiences.

Of course, *Pray Now* is generally used by individuals in their personal and private devotions; and, while that quiet space and time are important, the committee wanted to remind users and explore with them the fact that God is most often felt close where 'two or three are gathered' – where human beings engage with each other and discover in being together who we truly are. Perhaps therefore some meditations from the book this year could be used in groups at home or in the local church to help people reflect on some of the issues raised.

Journey with us as biblical groups teach about beautiful human traits such as hospitality, compassion and support, as well as illustrate the negative things that people are capable of when they come together in groups: oppression, prejudice and exclusion. How do we relate to each other in the groups we move within today? How do we belong together and connect with each other in such a diverse society? The Bible helps us understand as it offers us models of relationship and life in community and reminds us that God has created us to be together. *Pray Now 2006*, in text and illustration, helps us reflect on our need to give and receive love in colourful groups of varying shapes and sizes.

GAYLE TAYLOR
Convener of the Pray Now Group

Using this Book

A monthly cycle

This book provides material for prayer, meditation and study for each day of the month. In each new month, then, the cycle begins again. It is hoped that the material is so written that it is possible to return several times in this way and discover something new. The newness will be not necessarily be from the material but from ourselves.

However, some features will help users to 'move on' rather than simply go over old ground. For one thing, a variety of readings are offered. It is not intended that all of these are used at any one time but that, perhaps, one only is read. Titles given to each passage help us to choose what we will read that day.

Again, the prayer activity is designed so that, on returning again to one that has been used the previous month, we may find ourselves with an entirely new experience of prayer, even though beginning from the same starting point.

The illustrations are also meant to provide food for thought, and for prayer.

During the period of this edition, the new hymn book, the *Church Hymnary: Fourth Edition*, will increasingly be used. To acknowledge this, some of the 'blessings' are taken from hymns from this book, referred to throughout as *CH4*.

Prayer for the Church

Each day, there is prayer for some aspect of the work of the Church universal. The example given in *italics* refers to that area of work as it is carried forward in the Church of Scotland, but it is expected that those from other branches of the Church will substitute their own material. Again, at the end of the book there is a list of Church of Scotland Mission Partners, each with the day given on which they are to be prayed for. Members of other branches of the Church may wish to substitute similar persons or topics for prayer at that point.

The material should be used not slavishly but in the way that is most helpful. You may, for example, wish to substitute other prayers or readings, including the Lord's Prayer.

A daily lectionary

Included as an appendix is a separate list of daily Bible readings, based on the Scripture passages used in Church on Sunday by congregations that follow the lectionary in *Common Order* (the internationally used Revised Common Lectionary). This daily version is taken from a Uniting Church in Australia publication, *With Love to the World*, which also includes notes on the readings. Information about obtaining this publication is included with the list of readings.

Bulk buying

A price reduction may be applied when congregations or presbyteries purchase multiple copies of *Pray Now*. Further information may be had from the Office for Worship and Doctrine, wordoc@cofscotland.org.uk, 0131-225 5722 ext. 359.

Days of the Month

THE PEOPLE OF BABEL

Come, let us build ourselves a city, and a tower with its top in the heavens.

~ Genesis 11:4 ~

One language,
yet we cannot understand each other;
one God,
yet we cannot worship as one;
one world,
yet we cannot live together.

Holy God,
with truth,
bring a little confusion to our well-ordered theology
that has us at each other's throats;
with grace,
bring a little chaos
to the exclusive orthodoxy that divides us;
with love,
bring a little disorder
to the ingrained traditions
that prevent us from meeting each other.

And may we find the space to pray:
for those who live with division,
for those who cannot get along,
for those who arrive at conflict too easily,
and for those who do not understand.

One language,
and may we praise you with it;
one God,
and may we adventure together;
one world,
and may we share it lovingly.

Readings

Genesis 11:1–9	*The Tower of Babel*
Psalm 133	*Living in peace*
John 17:1–26	*Jesus prays*
1 Corinthians 1:10–17	*Divisions in the Church*
1 Corinthians 12:12–31	*One body, many parts*
Ephesians 4:1–16	*The unity of the body*

Prayer Activity

Reflect on an image of a tree and all its branches tangled together. Yet in this entanglement lies its beauty. Or consider a photograph of a range of mountains and its cragginess. In your mind, draw out its beauty from the roughness. Reflect finally on the confusions that may lie within your own life, and offer yourself space to look more from the eyes of God and imagine the deep-down beauty that God sees. Share in that encouragement.

Prayer for the Church

Its mission partners working with churches overseas and sharing their concerns (see page 75) and those who work in this country to support church and people in other countries and to remove crippling debt

especially the HIV/AIDS Project, Jubilee Scotland and aid agencies.

Blessing

May today offer a place of peace,
a moment of grace,
and many handfuls of love.

NOAH AND HIS FAMILY

*The Lord said to Noah, 'Go into the ark, you and all your
household, for I have seen that you alone are righteous
before me in this generation.'*

~ Genesis 7:1 ~

O Lord God, as children we loved the story of Noah's Ark:
  of the animals going in two by two,
  of the flood coming up and the rain coming down,
  of only eight being saved – the faithful Noah and his
  family.
Help us, as adults, to go on loving this story
  but also to understand it –
  that, though you can be scunnered with humanity, your
  mercy avails;
  that, though you can destroy, you can also save.
As we confess that we do not always find favour in your eyes,
  set the Cross between our souls and our sins;
  make us righteous in your sight.
Remind us that by Baptism we are saved through water,
  and that by your love in Christ we are called into your
  company,
  the ark royal that is the Church Catholic.
Stir the Church when she is too comfortably becalmed;
  steady her when storm and flood might overwhelm her;
  maintain her on true course in the present as in the past;
  and drive her by the power of the Spirit onward to your
  future.
O Lord God, today we remember
  all who go to sea in ships:
those serving in the Royal Navy and on merchant ships ...
  those fishing from our shores ...
  protect them from rock and tempest, fire and foe;
  be with all in peril on the sea.
  Support, we ask, all who strive for safety at sea ... all
  engaged in rescue ... all who minister to mariners.
Lord God, remember us,
  keep us true to our Baptism and safely on board the ark of
  salvation ...

learning our role in the company of Christ,
faithfully playing our part,
caring for your creatures great and small,
sending forth doves of peace into our troubled world.
AMEN.

Readings

Genesis 6:5–13	*The righteousness of Noah*
Genesis 6:14–7:16	*Noah builds the ark*
Genesis 7:17–8:14	*After the flood*
Genesis 8:15–22	*Leaving the ark*
Genesis 9:1–29	*God's rainbow, a sign of promise*
1 Peter 3:18–22	*Noah and our Baptism*

Prayer Activity

Think of someone whom you might help into the Ark that is the Church. Can you say 'Come along with me'? Do you really welcome a stranger who has come on board? Try to put prayers into action.

Prayer for the Church

Those who speak for the Church and show the relevance of the Gospel for our life in society

especially the Church and Society Council and the Scottish Churches' Parliamentary Office.

Blessing

Bless us, O God, when we are scunnered with the world
and with others;
enable us to trace the rainbow through the rain,
to remember your promises in and for nature,
and specially for the everlasting covenant,
in Jesus Christ who calls us into his company.　AMEN.

HEBREW ANCESTORS

*Again Jesus spoke to them, saying, 'I am the light of the
world. Whoever follows me will never walk in darkness
but will have the light of life.'*

~ John 8:12 ~

God of Abraham and Isaac and Jacob,
God of Columba and Queen Margaret and John Knox,
thank you for our heritage, for our connection with those
    who have gone before,
who have blazed the trail for us and made us aware
    that there is a Living Presence to follow,
    here in our land, on these shores.

Help us to learn from the way the Hebrews looked at time.
For them, the past was ahead of them, drawing them
    onwards, inspiring, stories to guide –
and always a shining light in their ancestors,
    glowing through them,
a consciousness that was bigger than one person,
    a light that shone,
a glorious radiance that their forefathers and foremothers
    embodied
but was bigger than any one person …

Like a desert caravan, following the one in front,
we are indeed part of a journey so much bigger than we can
    understand.
The caravan moves, but the whole earth is moving also.
We join with the caravan itself,
drawn by forces beyond our conception.

Enable us to be people who see the Christ light
    in the people of faith who have gone before
    and with whom we feel a resonance across space and time.
Entrust us to have courage that our vision is part of their
    vision.

Keep us faithful to that light.

Readings

Genesis 48	*One generation to the next*
1 Kings 2:1–12	*David sleeps with his ancestors*
Psalm 78	*God of our ancestors*
Luke 9:28–36	*Jesus meets his ancestors*
Acts 13:30–9	*God's promises to our ancestors*

Prayer Activity

Imagine a light shining through your heart connecting you to parents and grandparents and beyond. Follow that light within you in your imagination – see where it takes you or what it brings to light for you.

Prayer for the Church

Those who monitor developments in human knowledge and bring the insights of the Gospel to bear so that new discoveries might be used wisely

especially the Society, Religion and Technology Project and the Eco-congregation Project.

Blessing

May the light that flows in and through Jesus
lighten your path,
lift your burdens and worries,
connect you with the light of God
within you.

JOSEPH AND HIS BROTHERS

*But when his brothers saw that their father loved him
more than all his brothers, they hated him, and could not
speak peaceably to him.*

~ Genesis 37:4 ~

Creator of Love,
you know how we need to be loved.
You know that we need to feel special, nurtured and
    encouraged,
welcomed and one of the family.
So you gave us each other: to belong together,
    to connect with each other,
to be in relationship – understood and loved.

But God, you also know how complicated love gets.
How hard it is to be open and vulnerable
    – love might not be mutual.
How tiring it is to keep on loving
    – love might not be returned.
How painful it is to share love
    – love might be lost.

And, God, you know the thin line between love and hate.

Like Joseph and his brothers, we live in families
    that mix love and hate and indifference.
We often can't bring ourselves
    to speak peaceably to those closest to us.
Sometimes we say nothing
    – and our actions speak for themselves.

Forgive us, God. Teach us how to be together.
Show us a way through, with the bigger perspective
    that Jesus had as people loved and hated him.
Reassure us that, if we follow Christ, one day we will know
    reconciliation, deep peace and unconditional love.

Readings

Prayer Activity

Think of a family feud, a relative or friend you haven't seen for a long time. Remember your last meeting together – was that a good way to leave things? Has your perspective changed over time? Ask God to help you be the bigger person and if possible make the first move.

Prayer for the Church

Those who witness to the living Christ in the midst of his people, in Word and Sacrament, those who as deacons lead the Church in living out the Gospel, and those who recruit, train and support them

especially the Ministries Council.

Blessing

May the unconditional love of God
be realised in you and shown by you,
this day and every day.   AMEN.

SLAVES IN EGYPT

If only we had died by the hand of the Lord in the land of Egypt.

~ Exodus 16:3 ~

The restrictions, the checkpoints,
the reprisals, the put-downs,
the relentless discomfort, the beyond tiredness,
the lack of dignity
which affects our relationship
even with those in the same predicament,
not least wives, husbands, children,
when we ask ourselves –
Is there not something we could have done?
Could do? With a bit of get-up-and-go?

Lord, we pray for whole peoples today
who live under restrictions,
as minorities in their own land,
or exiled in refugee camps,
or as conquered peoples with only their memories
of a nation that was once great.
We pray for people who are victims of circumstance:
    asylum-seekers in our land tied to a gangmaster,
    nannies from abroad who are taken advantage of,
    sex workers lured under false pretences,
    sweat-shop labourers choosing slavery or starvation,
when to speak out is to find oneself on the next flight.

Is there something, Lord, of the slave mentality in us –
like Moses' followers wishing themselves back again
in the security of not having to take responsibility?
And are we not in thrall to the sinful impulses that drive us,
security-tagged so that we cannot escape ourselves?
And was not this why Christ came,
throwing wide the gates and inviting us to risk life with him,
travelling together to the promised land?

Readings

Exodus 1:8–14	*Taskmasters were appointed*
Exodus 16:1–12	*If only we had died*
Psalm 114	*Out of Egypt*
Daniel 1:1–7	*Fitted for service*
Galatians 4:1–11	*Slaves and heirs*
Ephesians 6:1–9	*Masters and slaves*

Prayer Activity

Is there any negative thing in your life that you hope God will never remove because you cannot do without it – a problem, attitude of mind, bad habit? Imagine life without it. Ask God to help you find a way through the desert – and take the first step today.

Prayer for the Church

The Church as it takes shape in areas where there are special difficulties – social, economic or health-related

especially for the work of the Priority Areas Committee.

Blessing

For everyone born, a place at the table,
to live without fear, and simply to be,
to work, to speak out, to witness and worship,
for everyone born, the right to be free.

Shirley Erena Murray
from *CH4*, no. 685

EGYPTIANS AND BABYLONIANS

Now they told David, 'The Philistines are fighting against Keilah, and are robbing the threshing floors.'

~ 1 Samuel 23:1 ~

There are times when I weigh up my life –
and among the many blessings
lie times of darkness
where I have been hurt,
or caught in some memory I cannot be rid of,
caused by a pain that oppresses me
of an uncaring word or selfish act of someone else.
It seems to scar memory
and crush all love.

And then I recall the times I too have unthinkingly
    oppressed others
with language that is careless,
actions that are selfish,
beliefs that are narrow.

And I consider all the things that drain life from people,
rather than offer them a blessing.

God of this day,
in this world where there is too much taking,
and not enough giving,
may I give a little more today.

Where oppression takes life,
may I give it back again
with words of encouragement or acts of kindness, like yours.
When prejudice binds up life,
may I free it again
with grace-filled compassion and gentle acceptance, like
    yours.

God, in all the places my life takes me,
help me redress the balance,
opening the door to freedom
and giving shape to grace.

Readings

Exodus 3:1–10	*The call of Moses*
Deuteronomy 26:1–11	*Remembering the past*
Hosea 11:1–10	*God repenting*
Psalm 12	*A prayer for help*
Luke 4:1–13	*The Kingdom manifesto*
Romans 8:1–17	*Life in the Spirit*

Prayer Activity

Take a look through the newspaper today, focus on one particular story, and reflect on it now and find some space at other times during the day. Ask questions about yourself such as 'How do I feel about this?'; 'What would it mean if this person was me or I was in the situation?' Write a few thoughts across the story symbolising the hope in which you pray for the situation.

Prayer for the Church

Those who ensure that the local church is well supported and staffed and who take initiatives in mission and outreach where people live, work and take leisure

especially the education/nurture and mission/evangelism task groups, and chaplaincies in hospitals, education, industry, prisons and residential homes.

Blessing

May your soul find a new step and the freedom to dance it.
May your spirit find a new emotion and the freedom to
    experience it.
May your heart find a new song and the freedom to sing it.
And may all of your life be lived in the freedom of love.

THE LEVITES

*At that time the Lord set apart the tribe of Levi to carry
the ark of the covenant of the Lord, to stand before the
Lord to minister to him, and to bless in his name, to
this day.*

~ Deuteronomy 10:8 ~

Lord, they were the professionals,
the temple administrators,
the religious establishment.

Descended from Aaron,
they had a lofty pedigree
as those charged with guarding the Law
and communicating the Faith to the people.

Yet how easily the system took over.
That which should have liberated people for living
became a constricting cage of conformity.
That which should have eased the burden
added ever greater loads to weary shoulders.

In its rigidity and its fear-driven defensiveness,
the establishment became a bulwark against the Kingdom,
a solid wall against change and newness.
It became an attempt to pin down the God
who is very Spirit and Life.

Lord, I pray for your Church
that has so often gone the same way
as the Temple and its officials.

I pray for those who are called to proclaim the Word
and to break the bread and pour the wine.
I pray for all who are charged with caring for the Church
and maintaining its life and witness in the community.

I pray for my own congregation and my part in it.

Readings

Genesis 29:31–5	*The birth of Levi*
Luke 10:29–37	*A Levite who walked by*
Deuteronomy 10:6–9	*The duties of the Levites*
Hebrews 7:1–14	*Christ: our Great High Priest*
Exodus 4:10–17	*Moses' brother: Aaron the Levite*

Prayer Activity

If you can, set aside a corner for prayer. In this place set two things: a dead twig and a flowering plant.

Sit in silence, looking at these objects. Ask yourself: what is the 'dead wood' in my life that needs to be discarded? Old resentments? Guilt? Prejudices? Offer these to God.

What are the signs of newness and fruitfulness in my life? Where is my life 'blossoming'? Give thanks to God for these signs of life.

Prayer for the Church

As it explores and renews its faith in the contemporary context and lifts the world and its people to God in praise and prayer

especially the worship and doctrine task group, all who lead and plan worship, and those who study and write about what Christians believe.

Blessing

Journey on in peace, in love and hope, in the knowledge that you are held in the encircling, upholding and enfolding Love of God, this day and for ever.   AMEN.

SPIES

The Lord said to Moses, 'Send men to spy out the land of Canaan, which I am giving to the Israelites.'

~ Numbers 13:1 ~

Lord, how often has humankind claimed that you have told them
to take the land you have given them and to fight their enemies?

The Old Testament is full of stories where we are told:
'God says' go, take, fight and kill.

We recognise that today leaders still claim your authority
for the wars they wage against our so-called 'enemies'.

We still send spies on secret intelligence-gathering missions;
we are still afraid to trust each other
and accept that each is different.

We forget that you created all life in all its variety;
we forget that Jesus commanded us to love our enemies.

How long do we need to continue to act out of fear?
How long do we need to continue to spy on our neighbour?
How long do we need to covet our neighbour's land?
How long do we need to oppress and exploit?

Loving God, help us to wrestle with the difficult decisions
that need to be made about intelligence and security.
Help us to see the bigger picture without blinkers
    seeing only our own small situation in life.
You sent Jesus to show us the way;
help us to trust in you and not to be afraid.   AMEN.

Readings

Genesis 42:1–25	*Joseph's brothers go to Egypt*
Numbers 13	*Spies report on the Promised Land*
Numbers 14	*Rebellion, intercession, disobedience*
Joshua 2	*Spies sent to Jericho*
1 Samuel 26	*David spares Saul's life*
Luke 20:20–6	*Spies sent to trap Jesus*

Prayer Activity

We all 'spy' and gather information on a daily basis, sometimes publicly, sometimes privately behind the curtains. What do we do with that information? Do we use it to make our world and our own communities a better place, or do we abuse it and use it for evil purposes? Ponder for a moment what you did with the last piece of information you gathered, and quietly tell God about it.

Prayer for the Church

As it retells the story of the Gospel for our time, reaching those who have never heard and refreshing those who have heard it all before

especially the Scottish Story-Telling Centre and the wider work of the Netherbow.

Blessing

Father, bless your wayward children,
Jesus, love us when we fail,
Spirit, guide us on our way.

THE GIDEONITES

*Not to us, O Lord, not to us, but to your name give glory
… You who fear the Lord, trust in the Lord!
He is their help and shield.*

~ Psalm 115:1a and 11 ~

Lord God, we praise you; you are indeed our help and shield!
When things were hard for old Israel, you raised up Gideon,
     giving him a sign, endowing him with courage.
So it has been down through history:
     'Cometh the hour, cometh the man.'
Robert Bruce … John Knox … Horatio Nelson … Winston
     Churchill …
     who brought life and liberty to the nation.
Praise be! You also raised up men and women
     for that other nation:
     the new Israel; the Church of Christ –
Columba … Margaret … Alexander Henderson … Thomas
     Chalmers … George MacLeod.

Lord God, we remember also the relative few
     who have done so much:
Gideon's three hundred, who with spiritual courage, by skilful
     ruse and with brave cry
     defeated the Midianites and helped restore Israel to you;
the twelve disciples who became apostles …
the Reformation martyrs like Wishart and the gentle
     Patrick Hamilton,
     '*whose reek infected as many as it blew upon*';
the hardy Scottish Covenanters like Peden and Renwick
          who proclaimed '*the crown rights of the Redeemer*';
and in recent times
     'the Few' who in the Battle of Britain saved our nation.

Lord God, raise us up, if not to be like Gideon,
     yet to be one of the 'Gideonites'
     willing to rise and respond to your call:
     to do and dare; in faith, in love, in hope.   AMEN.

Readings

Judges 6:11–40   *Gideon looks for a sign*
Judges 7   *The Gideonites defeat the Midianites*
Judges 8:1–32   *Gideon triumphs further*

Prayer Activity

'Whom shall I send?' Do you answer: 'Send someone else!'? Think of some talent, maybe great, maybe quite small, that could be of use in the service of the Lord. Ask if you want to remain among the many or dare to join the few, that precious few.

Prayer for the Church

Those who bring their creativity to bear on making known the Gospel, in print, film, news media, sound and website

especially Saint Andrew Press, Life & Work, the Publishing Committee, and those who maintain the Church's website.

Blessing

Thus God our spirits lifts
fresh daring to inspire;
as common folk get gifts
to change the world entire:
    the tongues of flame at Pentecost
    run through the world like forest fire.

Ian M. Fraser
from *CH4*, no. 584

PHILISTINES

*Do not cease to cry out to the Lord our God for us,
and pray that he may save us from the hand of the
Philistines.*

~ 1 Samuel 7:8 ~

Lord, how do we know who your enemies are?
Were the Philistines really beyond the pale?
Were they not defending their land and livelihood?
Are they not more like us than we allow?
No-one likes philistines.
For us they have become a byword;
they cause opera houses to close,
believe function comes before beauty;
anyway, that's the way we see them.
But might we be seeing an expression of a different culture,
rather than no culture at all?

Lord, we are not only content to be right;
the other person has to be wrong.
As nations, we need others who are not us
so that we have an identity to cling to.
Save us from demonising whole peoples
just because we need there to be a difference
between them and us,
so that when we consume, when we hoard,
we can say: 'Because we're worth it!
We need have no conscience about these others!'

Help us, Lord, not to use culture or custom
as a means of identity, defining who we are,
but to slip as effortlessly as Christ
into the lives and lifestyles of others,
at home with them, one family.
Give us the generosity that offers all we have,
as Christ gave all for us.

Readings

1 Samuel 17	*David and the Philistine champion*
Romans 5:1–11	*Once we were God's enemies*
Galatians 3:23–9	*One in Christ Jesus*
Luke 6:20–38	*Turning the other cheek*
Matthew 26:6–13	*A generous gesture*

Prayer Activity

Do you know people from another country or culture? Or from another part of the UK now in your community or church? Think of one of these. Ask what makes him or her different from you. Then ask if there is anything you have in common.

Prayer for the Church

Those who bring care and encouragement to people in any kind of need and who work for a healthier society in which all may find fulfilment

especially the Social Care Council, CrossReach, and the staff of the various units it operates.

Blessing

Not on this land alone,
but be God's mercies known
from shore to shore.
Lord, make the nation see
that all should kindred be,
and form one family
the world o'er.

W. E. Hickson, third verse of National Anthem
from *CH4*, no. 703

EXILES

*I will put my spirit within you, and you shall live, and
I will place you on your own soil; then you shall know
that I, the Lord, have spoken and will act.*

~ Ezekiel 37:14 ~

For those who grieve the separation of exile,
for those far from home who know they will not be back,
for those who have long since given up
    expecting that you will speak and you will act,
my spirit calls out to you, God, in prayer.

Home is where the heart is – but where is your heart, God?
Surely with the wanderers in the wilderness – although they
    do not know it.
With the asylum-seeker and the terminal patient who want to
    be somewhere else,
somewhere better, somewhere promised?
God, surely your heart is within us –
beating for those whom globalisation has made into
    outsiders
stirring for those excluded from comfort, dignity and peace,
longing for those estranged and distant to be close again.

So let your heart pulse within us now,
carrying life to every dry and barren land,
inspiring people to get up, believe and hope once more.
Help us return to you, God, help us find the kingdom where
    we are
and move us to see and touch and hear where we belong
    – with you.

Readings

Ezekiel 37:1–14	*The valley of dry bones*
2 Kings 17:22–3	*Sinful Israel is exiled*
Luke 15:11–32	*The Prodigal returns*

Prayer Activity

Think of a time when you have been away from home, perhaps on business or holiday. What do you look forward to coming back to, what helps you feel that you have really returned home? Reflect on this, and the next time you experience this be aware of all it means, giving God your thanks.

Prayer for the Church

Those who help us to take our place in, and be enriched by, the experience and witness of the Church throughout the world

especially the World Mission Council, Scottish Churches' World Exchange, and St Colm's International House, Edinburgh.

Blessing

> Love is the light in the tunnel of pain;
> love is the will to be whole once again;
> love is the trust of a friend on the road;
> God is where love is, for love is of God.

Alison Robertson
from *CH4*, no. 115

BUILDERS OF THE TEMPLE

Unless the Lord builds the house, those who build it labour in vain.

~ Psalm 127:1 ~

Lord, we thank you for those sacred places
 where your Word is declared, your Sacraments
  administered,
 when we sensed that you were there, when a fellowship
  was enjoyed,
 where and when we really worshipped you,
 where and when your grace was given.
We thank you for the many whose giving and doing
 built the kirks of our land;
 for the many whose praising, preaching and praying
  hallowed their walls;
 for the many who in times past built our towns and cities:
 architects and engineers, masons and bricklayers, and
  many more.

Recalling those who, with Nehemiah, restored the Temple of
 Jerusalem,
 raise up in our day builders like Nehemiah's
 to repair and to create new sacred spaces.
Strengthen us to be the Church without walls,
 breaking through barriers for the good of the Gospel.
 Make us living stones in that great enterprise.
Lord, as we commend to you all who strive for a Jerusalem
 on earth:
 statesmen and sociologists, economists and planners of all
  kinds;
 watch over the watchmen: those in the police and
  emergency services;
 and strengthen the hands of those who would do a good
  work for your Kingdom.   AMEN.

Readings

Prayer Activity

> Remember the children's question, 'Are you a stumbling block or a stepping stone?' Or, 'Are you a real brick?' Think how you may help others and the Other; how you might play a better part in the fabric of society and in building up the Church – and don't be afraid of being used!

Prayer for the Church

Those who seek to renew the life and mission of the Church, develop strategies and establish priorities

especially the Council of Assembly, the Panel for Renewal and Reform, and the Church without Walls initiative.

Blessing

May the blessing of the Father, the great creator,
the blessing of Christ the Son, the divine carpenter,
the blessing of the Holy Spirit, the inspirer
be with us.   AMEN.

FALSE PROPHETS

*Now therefore have all Israel assemble for me at Mount
Carmel, with the four hundred and fifty prophets of Baal
and the four hundred prophets of Asherah, who eat at
Jezebel's table.*

~ 1 Kings 18:19 ~

When I read this story, it wakes me up
to how great was the revolution you brought, O Christ.
Like Elijah you listened to God and obeyed,
but hundreds and thousands of people
were *not* killed in the name of God.

You pointed us to the battles within our own hearts.
You indicated that this is where to put our fighting energies,
conquering our inner violence,
learning the skilful difficult way
of loving our enemies … and ourselves.

What a radical shift of perspective.

As Elijah was given Elisha as companion
as the one who continued the prophetic line,
you give us your living Holy Spirit
to continue your living presence here and now.
We are your hands and feet and mind.

So help us now in the name of God
to know how to stand against people who stand against our
    faith.
Grant us deep wisdom to be warriors for peace.

Listening for your living voice,
guiding us to your ways for now,
we trust that in Christ's name
we can leave behind choices of magic and bloodshed.

Readings

Deuteronomy 13:1–5	*Test the prophets*
I Kings 18:1–46	*Elijah with the prophets of Baal*
I Kings 19:1–21	*The effects on Elijah*
Matthew 7:12–23	*Jesus' words on prophets*
John 6:41–51	*Jesus' reaction to complaints*

Prayer Activity

All of us have the potential to be violent. Name now before Christ an area of your inner world where you experience violent feelings, angry feelings, or conflicts or confusions. Have the courage to ask the Holy Spirit to help you look at these more deeply. Notice particularly how these affect your body – usually bringing physical tension. Notice where in your body. Ask Christ for healing both of the origins and of the effects in your body.

Prayer for the Church

As it meets in councils and assemblies to listen to God and one another

especially the Assembly Arrangements Committee, the Nomination Committee, the Moderator, the Moderator Designate, the Principal Clerk and the Depute Clerk.

Blessing

> Drop thy still dews of quietness
> till all our strivings cease.
> Take from our souls the strain and stress
> and let our ordered lives confess
> the beauty of thy peace.

John Greenleaf Whittier
from *CH4*, no. 485

TRUE PROPHETS

*Before I formed you in the womb I knew you, and before
you were born I consecrated you; I appointed you a
prophet to the nations.*

~ Jeremiah 1:5 ~

God of life and upheaval,
God of the devastating Word
and the appalling vision:

I thank you today for true prophets,
for those who were not at home
in the world as it was in their own day
but who lived passionately
for a world that was yet to be born.

I thank you today for those
who would not keep quiet
and who, regardless of the consequences,
refused to keep the vision locked away
within their own hearts.

I thank you today for those
who look out upon the world
with the double vision of the prophet:
who see the world in all its pain and mess
and yet also see it as you would have it be.

Lord, teach me to see as you do.
Open my eyes.   AMEN.

Readings

Jeremiah 1:1–10   *The calling of a prophet*
Matthew 4:12–17   *Prophecy fulfilled in Jesus*
Jeremiah 31:31–4   *A new Covenant prophesied*
Luke 19:41–4   *Jesus laments what might have been*
Amos 2:4–8   *The prophet denounces social injustice*
Matthew 12:33–7   *Judge them by their fruit*

Prayer Activity

> Using photographs or political cartoons cut from
> magazines and newspapers, make a wallchart (or
> scrapbook) of prophetic double vision. On one side
> you might have images of injustice, war, oppression,
> greed, hunger and so on. On the other side you might
> have images of healing, of compassion, of community,
> of co-operation and of rebuilding. Use these images as
> a focus for your prayers.

Prayer for the Church

Those who guide and administer the details of the Church's
life at national level

especially the Central Services Committee, personnel
bodies, committees and trustees for pensions, investments
and housing.

Blessing

The love of Christ keep you strong in service, the passion
of Christ keep you bold in caring, and the patience of
Christ keep you active in waiting for the dawning of the
Kingdom.   AMEN.

THE PSALMISTS

I love you, O Lord, my strength.

~ Psalm 18:1 ~

Their voices rise from the pages of Scripture,
the greatest choir of all history,
putting praise in the mouths of all who followed,
bringing even creation to utterance,
providing the sounds that surrounded a Saviour,
as he grew, ministered, died and rose:
'God is gone up with a shout,
the Lord with the sound of a trumpet.'

Lord, show me how to look at the world,
so that your praise will be on my lips also.
Help me like the psalmists to see you in all things,
in the good, the bad and the ugly;
help me like them to be honest before you,
able to ask questions, to complain,
to plead, but also to trust you completely,
as my Rock, my refuge, my defence, my comforter.

Hear my prayer for those among God's people
who make music, and enable others to make music,
but those who praise too in stone and wood,
in movement, and lives of service,
in vows of silence instead of verses of song;
and those also who castigate God –
who lament for the suffering in the world
and demand that it cease.

Readings

Psalm 138	*With my whole heart*
Psalm 139	*How can I escape you?*
Psalm 142	*I pour out my complaint*
Colossians 3:12–17	*Sing from the heart*
Mark 14:26–31	*The Passover psalm*

Prayer Activity

> Everyone has a song – not a favourite that someone else has written, but the song that is yours alone, that expresses your personality, faith, outlook on the world. What is the main theme of your song? What would the melody that should go with it sound like – joyous, melancholy, repetitive? If you like, hum it.

Prayer for the Church

Those who guide the Church in temporal matters and see that in its dealings justice prevails

especially the Law Department.

Blessing

> For the love of my friends and kin
> I will bless you with signs of peace.
> For the love of God's own people
> I will labour and pray for you.

Psalm 122, verse 5, Bernadette Farrell
from *CH4*, no. 83

NATIVITY VISITORS

Do not be afraid: for see – I am bringing you good news of great joy for all the people: to you is born this day in the city of David a Saviour, who is the Messiah, the Lord.

~ Luke 2:10–12 ~

Human God,
when we think about your birth, we have to remind
    ourselves that you, become flesh,
were in our world, in a manger, in a stable.
You were outside the comforts of hotel or inn,
outside in the cold and the dirt,
outwith the 'normal' family set-up –
painfully born into human experience
so that we may make our way painfully back to God.

And when that news sank in, Human God,
the world was amazed at love come down –
you, actually here with us!
You walked where we walk, saw what we see,
felt what we felt.
Those shepherds rejoiced in that – one of us, God with us!

But the good news to the poor didn't stop there,
for soon the rich wise men knelt down amazed too.

Today, as we remember the story of your birth, Human God,
whoever we are, whatever we are and wherever we are in
    life,
we give you our thanks for sharing our humanity.
Let us hear the angels sing, see that you are holy
and learn to kneel down.

Readings

Isaiah 9:2–7	*Those in darkness see light*
Luke 2:8–20	*The shepherds and the angels*
Matthew 2:1–12	*Visitors from the east*

Prayer Activity

In many church traditions, kneeling is a position used for prayer. If you can, try this position today; how does your perspective/sense of being change as you do this? If you do not wish to kneel, think of times when you have seen others kneel, and reflect on the significance of this with God.

Prayer for the Church

Those who care for members of the armed forces as they seek to preserve peace in the world

especially the Chaplains' Committee.

Blessing

Love Divine, all loves excelling,
joy of heaven to earth come down,
fix in us thy humble dwelling...
enter every trembling heart.

Charles Wesley
from *CH4*, no. 519

THE ANAWIM*

*My soul waits for the Lord more than those who watch
for the morning.*

~ Psalm 130:6a ~

They were called the Anawim.
Were they not the humble ones,
the forgotten and powerless ones?

Yet in their openness and poverty of spirit,
in their simplicity and faith,
they were the great ones in your eyes, Lord,
the powerful ones, the key players in your story.

I remember those who, like Mary and Joseph,
Simeon and Anna, kept alight the lamp of faith
when others had given way to cynicism
or had settled into quiet despair.

They were there as your sentinels,
alert and responsive to your Word,
keenly scanning the dark horizon
for signs of your Kingdom's dawning.

Lord, I pray for your Anawim across the world,
the humble faithful who refuse to abandon hope,
for those who have glimpsed a reddening in the sky
and who are active in waiting for your coming.

* *plural form of an Old Testament word, translated in various ways
as 'poor', 'afflicted', 'humble' or 'meek'. The anawim were the faithful
remnant, the powerless ones, whose only resource was God. The main
characters in the first two chapters of Luke's Gospel could all be
characterised as 'Anawim'.*

Readings

Luke 1:46–56	*Mary's prayer*
Zephaniah 2:1–3, 3:11–13	*The faithful remnant*
Luke 2:25–38	*Simeon and Anna*
Isaiah 41:17–20	*The poor and needy ones*
Matthew 5:3–12	*The Beatitudes*
Luke 2:8–14	*The Shepherds*
Psalm 130	*The song of the faithful ones*

Prayer Activity

Read the story of Simeon and Anna. Picture the scene in the Temple. Visualise the facial expressions of Mary, Joseph, Simeon and Anna, the infant Jesus. What emotions do they show? Wonder? Fear and foreboding? Confusion? Hope? Longing? Think of people known to you (or featured in the news) whose situations reflect these emotions. Pray for them.

Prayer for the Church

The organisations of women and men who worship, study and take the lead in reaching out to others

especially the Church of Scotland Guild.

Blessing

God of the humble and powerless
make you strong in gentleness and mighty in mercy,
this day, this week and into all eternity.   AMEN.

DISCIPLES

*And Jesus said to them, 'Follow me and I will make you
fish for people.' And immediately they left their nets and
followed him.*

~ Mark 1:17–18 ~

Lord Jesus, you said 'Follow me' and they did;
the twelve chosen to be your closest disciples,
and others, adding their experience to the group.

Today we reflect on this assortment of people from everyday
    walks of life,
none of them highly educated or religious,
nothing particularly special about them.

Yet, Lord, you saw their potential;
you saw past the labels of tax-collector and fisherman,
you saw in them what they could and would be.

It would have been wonderful to be a fly on the wall
listening to all their conversations and discussions:
what did they speak about in private?
were they always serious?
did they have a laugh every now and then?
what were their private thoughts about you,
Jesus, whom they followed?

You see the potential in each of us
and call us to 'come and follow'.
Help us to leave everything behind
and immediately follow you, today and every day.

Readings

Mark 1:16–20	*Calling of the first disciples*
John 1:43–51	*Jesus calls Philip and Nathanael*
Matthew 10:1–15	*The twelve disciples' mission*
Mark 9:30–7	*Fear and rivalry*
Luke 8:22–5	*Lack of faith*
John 8:31–59	*True disciples*

Prayer Activity

> The disciples were fortunate in that they could speak to Jesus in person, face to face. Close your eyes and imagine that you are sitting with Jesus. Is there something you would like to talk to him about? Tell him now and sit quietly, enjoying being in his presence.

Prayer for the Church

Those who are concerned that the physical surroundings of the local church assist towards deeper worship, warmer hospitality and stronger witness

especially the Committee on Church Art and Architecture.

Blessing

Life-giving Father,
life-saving Jesus,
life-guiding Spirit,
bless us this day.

THE 5,000

We have nothing here but five loaves and two fish.
~ Matthew 14:17 ~

God, whose hands held the fish,
and tore the bread,
feed the hunger in me
for peace,
for justice,
for grace.

God, whose hands blessed the fish,
and broke the bread,
feed the hunger of the world
for balance,
for fairness,
for truthfulness.

God, in whose hands fish fed a multitude,
and bread delivered a banquet,
I come to you,
along with the world,
hungry for forgiveness,
and a new imperative,
where sharing becomes a sacred act,
where feeding the hungry shapes a sacrament,
and where banqueting with the world
is the substance of heaven.

Readings

Deuteronomy 8:1–3	*Manna in the wilderness*
Leviticus 23:22	*Harvesting*
Matthew 5:6	*Beatitudes*
Matthew 14:13–21	*Feeding the 5,000*
John 7:37–41	*Come to me*
1 Corinthians 11:23–25	*Lord's Supper*

Prayer Activity

> Find a photograph or an object that speaks to you about generosity. It may be an image of your friends or family, it may be a present someone gave you. Simply take some time to let these images or objects remind you about the generosity you've experienced in life in many different ways.

Prayer for the Church

Those who at all levels encourage and enable different branches of the Church to relate to and learn from each other and about the Gospel they share

especially the Committee on Ecumenical Relations as it operates through the new Councils and as it enables the Church to play its part in Action for Churches Together in Scotland and other national and international bodies through which Churches meet.

Blessing

May you feast on the banquet of love,
taste the exuberance of grace,
and be filled by the generosity of heaven,
today and every day.

DEMONS

Now the spirit of the Lord departed from Saul, and an evil spirit from the Lord tormented him.

~ 1 Samuel 16:14 ~

Lord, I want to model my life on you, love you, follow in
    your ways.
Help me when I feel as if there is a demon inside me –
like those times I find it impossible to control my thoughts
    or feelings,
or when I seem unable to stop myself from saying hurtful
    things
and I wonder why I feel so powerless.
When my anger, distress or confusion breaks into the open
and I, and others, see a side of myself I prefer to pretend is
    not there,
sometimes I experience this as if an enemy has got inside
    me, a demon.
Other times it is as if my emotions are controlling me.
Or are these the same thing?

I ask for your wisdom, your firmness and gentleness to
    prompt and teach me
to navigate the storms of my inner world
by listening to my emotions,
allowing your Spirit to teach me in the midst of them.

And I pray for people who live with particularly difficult
    emotional states,
asking for relief and release for them and, above all, hope.

I pray for people who help them, for your grace and blessing
    for them.
I ask for your help to discern with you how I need to take
    evil seriously,
to follow you with all my heart and mind and strength
and to learn to fear nothing.

In Jesus' name.

Readings

Prayer Activity

Think of a time when you had to wrestle with your emotions. What helped you to resolve the situation? Recognise how much help came from beyond your own resources.

Prayer for the Church

As it seeks new patterns of ministry and mission for the more effective use of personnel and a stronger interface with the community

especially new parish groupings and area team ministries.

Blessing

The guarding of the God of life be on you,
the guarding of the loving Christ be on you,
the guarding of the Holy Spirit be on you
to aid you and enfold you
each day and night of your lives.   AMEN.

Common Order, p. 597

PHARISEES, SADDUCEES, ZEALOTS

> *The Pharisees and the Sadducees came, and to test Jesus*
> *they asked him to show them a sign from heaven.*
>
> ~ Matthew 16:1 ~

Lord, there is something of the Pharisee in me:
sure that basically I am a good person
but not so sure about the others;
yet I need more of the Pharisees at their best:
    firmly focused on God,
    letting their religion shape their lives,
    fiercely dismissive of substitutes.

How difficult for Jesus to stand out
against people with right on their side,
so that he could offer more than they thought possible.
How difficult to contradict the Sadducees,
the establishment no-one questioned,
embedded in church and state.
How difficult not to throw in his lot with the Zealots,
passionate about freedom and liberty.
How daring to challenge the Scribes,
experts in religion, law and morals.

Give those who espouse causes,
who construct programmes for the good of all,
who want the best for everyone,
the grace and courage to examine themselves,
to be able to question and continually reassess
their goals and their motives,
and the quality of their love for others.

Readings

Matthew 16:1–12	*A warning to the disciples*
Mark 11:27–33	*Jesus is challenged*
Matthew 22:15–46	*Trick questions*
Matthew 23:15–36	*Blind guides*
Luke 6:1–11	*Flying in the face of authority*
Luke 18:10–13	*Pharisee and tax-collector*

Prayer Activity

> If you are like most, there will be some people you don't
> really approve of. Pick one of them and list their good
> points. Give thanks for these, then pray about the things
> in them you cannot like. Finally, ask God for honesty
> about the reasons that cause you to disapprove.

Prayer for the Church

Those who ensure that the fabric of church buildings is
maintained and that the Church's heritage in buildings is
conserved for the good of the Church and the nation

especially the General Trustees.

Blessing

> Lord, cleanse the depths within our souls,
> and bid resentment cease.
> Then, bound to all in bonds of love,
> our lives will spread your peace.

Rosamond Herklots
from *CH4*, no. 486

CROWDS AROUND JESUS

When he saw the crowds, he had compassion for them,
because they were harassed and helpless, like sheep
without a shepherd.

~ Matthew 9:36 ~

Lord Jesus, you knew all about crowds:
  you moved among them, you taught and healed them, you
    fed them even;
  they were often captivated by you:
  amazed at what you did, in awe of your authority,
    impressed by your words.
As we in our day sense you,
  may any fascination turn into faith, any wonder turn into
    worship.
As we hear you speak may we, like many long ago, hear you
    gladly,
  and may we acclaim you as the Palm Sunday crowd
    acclaimed you.
  Son of David, help us to go with the crowd, such a crowd
    as shouted 'Hosanna!'
Lord Jesus, you knew all about crowds:
  that other crowd who came with swords and clubs to
    arrest you,
  that other crowd who replied to Pilate's question as to
    what he might do,
  that crowd which shrieked 'Crucify! ... His blood be on us!'
Save us from going with such crowds:
  those who in blood lust seek supposed retribution,
  those who shout in nationalistic malice or sing some
    chauvinistic sinister song
  those who watching some exciting game express bitter
    bigotry in chant or chorus.

We pray for situations where men and women meet in
    large numbers:
  political demonstrations ... football matches ... pop
    festivals ... evangelistic meetings ...
  may there be enthusiasm with sense, excitement without
    danger, enjoyment unalloyed.

Lord Jesus, we pray for crowds and for ourselves when we
might be in them.
Let not panic take a grip, with folk creating their own
disaster.
So may they and we come to that crowd that no one can
number
who see you face to face in the Father's House.   AMEN.

Readings

Matthew 4:23–5	*Crowds follow Jesus*
Matthew 9:35–8	*Jesus' compassion for the crowds*
Matthew 21:1–11	*The Palm Sunday crowd*
Matthew 27:15–26	*The Good Friday crowd*
Luke 23:44–9	*The crowd come to gloat*
Revelation 7:9–17	*A multitude before the throne*

Prayer Activity

Imagine yourself in a great crowd and going with it
– would you lose control of the 'You' in you, letting
yourself be submerged or allowing yourself to be
elevated? To what extent do people, the media and the
fashion of the day take over your life? Realise as you
think about the freedom which God gives us and the
strength he can supply.

Prayer for the Church

The increasing number of people who choose to relate to
the Church less through traditional membership patterns and
more through general commitment and particular projects.

Blessing

As your Fatherly care marks the fall of a sparrow,
as Jesus your Son among the crowd noted Zacchaeus,
as your Spirit can touch each and every one of us,
bless us and keep us every one in your care
and number us among the saints now and forever.   AMEN.

THE SICK

And he cured many who were sick with various diseases.
~ Mark 1:34 ~

They came to you in great numbers, healing Christ,
because they wanted to be well.
They pushed in on you and clamoured at your feet –
not caring if you saw them touch you or not
so long as they were better.

And you came to them because 'those who are well have no
    need of a physician',
reminding us that our lack of sight, our discomfort in our
    own skin,
our inability to move and speak are linked to our separation
    from God.

Christ who brought healing, wholeness and hope,
we come to you now, wanting you to see the mess of our
    lives,
the brokenness of our world, the fragility of our bodies.
For like the lepers we desire to be clean,
like the blind we need to see things we've missed before,
and, like the woman who touched your cloak, we humbly
    approach you
hoping that our faith can make us well.

Lord, as we pray for those ill at home or in hospital today,
we pray too for ourselves as carers and prayers.
Because we believe – help our unbelief.

Readings

Matthew 9:20–7	*Touching the hem of Christ's cloak*
Matthew 12:9–14	*Healing on the Sabbath*
Luke 17:11–19	*Jesus heals ten men*
Mark 5:1–20	*Jesus heals a man with evil spirits*
Mark 10:46–52	*Blind Bartimaeus*

Prayer Activity

Sit quietly for a few moments. Listen to your breathing. Think of God as 'Holy Breath' and cherish how close God is to you. Now acknowledge that God is also as close as that to others, and in this moment remember those who are ill at home or in hospital.

Prayer for the Church

Those who steward the Church's financial resources and recall its members to the meaning of Christian giving

especially the Stewardship and Finance Committee and the General Treasurer's Department.

Blessing

Jesu, Jesu,
fill us with your love,
show us how to serve
the neighbours we have
from you.

Tom Colvin
from *Songs of God's People*, no. 60

WOMEN AROUND JESUS

Many women were also there, looking on from a distance;
they had followed Jesus from Galilee and had provided
for him.

~ Matthew 27:55 ~

Lord Jesus, when you walked the earth you didn't just call
    men;
you called women too and encouraged them to follow and
    learn from you.

Let us ponder for a moment on these women:
women who followed and provided for you.
They were fortunate, given an unusual opportunity
to leave their homes and follow their Messiah,
to walk and talk with you.

You made them the centre of attention, Jew or Gentile,
you healed them, had compassion for them,
discussed weighty matters with them
When you rose, it was to women that you first appeared.
Surely there can be no greater affirmation.

Still today women have continued to follow you,
sometimes quietly in the background, sometimes not so quietly.

Women today play many roles,
no longer just homemakers, wives and mothers, sisters and
    daughters.
We pray for women who still have to fight hard to be allowed
to step out of their homes and into all walks of life
to make their voices heard.

Readings

Luke 8:1–3	*Some women accompany Jesus*
Luke 7:36–50	*Jesus forgives a sinful woman*
Luke 24:1–12	*The resurrection of Jesus*
Matthew 9:18–26	*Life and healing*
Mark 7:24–30	*A Syrophoenician woman's faith*
John 2:1–12	*The wedding at Cana*

Prayer Activity

Think of the women who have been with you on your journey: mother, sister, friend, colleague. Take a moment to think of what makes these women special for you, then thank God for them and ask his blessing on them.

Prayer for the Church

Those who encourage and assist congregations to explore and develop patterns of life and mission appropriate to their own context

especially the Parish Development Fund Committee and the Scottish Churches Community Trust.

Blessing

In the love of God
may we be warmed and welcomed;
in the joy of Jesus
may we be strengthened and made whole;
in the breath of the Spirit
may we be challenged and blessed.

Ruth Burgess, *A Book of Blessings and How to Write your Own* (Wild Goose Publications, 2001), p. 121

TAX-COLLECTORS/SINNERS

Why does your teacher eat with tax-collectors and sinners?

~ Matthew 9:11 ~

I'm glad you did, Jesus,
eat with tax-collectors and sinners, that is.
I'm glad heaven makes space for outsiders
and that grace is shaped like a table
and invites the world to dine.
I'm glad you made friends with the conspiring,
the forgotten,
the broken,
the radicals,
that you went home with the terrorist and the fool,
for I find myself more at home there
than among the clean linen
and polished halos of the saints.

Such generosity is heaven's gift to the world,
such openness is heaven's desire for the world,
such willingness to hope is heaven's bounty to the world,
such radical inclusion is heaven's intent for the world,
such readiness to accept is heaven's language for the world,
such strength to love is heaven's justice in the world.

Eat with me, Jesus,
a banquet of inclusion,
and may my living,
my faith,
my love,
be as generous and as open,
as yours.

Readings

Matthew 5:1–12	*Radical inclusiveness*
Matthew 9:9–13	*The calling of Levi*
Matthew 11:27–29	*Heavy burdens*
Romans 5:7–9	*While we were still sinners*

Prayer Activity

Take a sheet of paper and draw a circle on it. Write around the circle groups of people, or names of indi-viduals, that the world excludes for one reason or another. Pray for them and, as you do, write the name of the group or the individual within the circle, symbolising their gathering into God's love.

Prayer for the Church

Those who offer special expertise to local congregations as they seek to develop their work, worship and witness

especially the Regional Development Officers of the Mission and Discipleship Council.

Blessing

May your door always be unlocked,
and your hallway always welcome.
May a light always be at your window,
and your table large enough to feed every guest.
May your wisdom be sharp enough to recognise every
     sinner,
and your love broad enough to make each an exception.

APOSTLES AT PENTECOST

In the last days it will be, God declares, that I will pour out my Spirit upon all flesh, and your sons and your daughters shall prophesy, and your young men shall see visions, and your old men shall dream dreams.

~ Acts 2:17 ~

Lord, I praise you for Pentecost
when fearful and faltering apostles
caught the hint of a new fragrance.
I praise you for those who knew
the south wind of your spirit,
breathing hope of Spring and new beginnings
into hearts clamped in Winter's grip
of agonising shame and failure.

I praise you that ordinary, all-too-frail
human beings just like me
realised to their utter astonishment
that they were no longer slaves
to the crippling pain of yesterday,
but were now liberated
into the energising promise of tomorrow.

I praise you for their discovery
that the last word
is not one of defeat but of victory,
that the Word that echoes into all eternity
is not 'My God, My God, why have you forsaken me?'
but 'Christ is risen – he is risen indeed!'

Today, Lord, I pray for the Church,
that we might take your springtime
into a world still in winter's grip.

Readings

Prayer Activity

In the Old Testament, the Hebrew word for *Spirit* is the same as that for breath or wind: *Ruach*. Sit upright in a chair, and gradually slow down your breathing by taking deeper and longer breaths. As you breathe in, imagine you are breathing in the Spirit of God – the Spirit of wholeness, of healing and of new life. As you breathe out, imagine that you are exhaling the poisons of bitterness, anger, resentment, fear and so on. You may find it helpful to use words (within yourself) such as I breathe in God's peace … I breathe out my anxiety, I breathe in God's compassion, I breathe out my selfishness, I breathe in God's hope, I breathe out my fears …

Prayer for the Church

As it meets in local Church councils where support is given and policies made

especially the Presbyteries, their Moderators and Clerks; Kirk Sessions and Session Clerks; Congregational Boards, Deacons' Courts and their Clerks.

Blessing

The Spirit of Pentecost, the breath of Christ, fill you with the knowledge of God and his purposes, that you might serve him this day* in joy and trust.   AMEN.

* *or* this night.

COURTS

Do not judge, so that you may not be judged. For with the judgement you make you will be judged, and the measure you give will be the measure you get.

~ Matthew 7:1–2 ~

Lord Jesus Christ, you were tried by various people and
    courts in Jerusalem;
help me to see, to realise, that somehow I too was there
    and still am!
There among the Scribes and Pharisees: the unco guid;
there, like Caiaphas and Annas, conscious of my power;
there in the courtyard with Peter, afraid for my own skin;
there with Pilate, recognising truth but wanting to keep
    my position;
there beside Herod, interested only in some entertainment;
there in the crowd: my voice adding to the cry of 'Crucify!'

Lord, my Judge and Saviour,
forgive me for my vanity and for my misuse of any power I
    may possess;
forgive me for my poor discipleship, for which if on trial as
    you were I might be convicted;
forgive me for any moral cowardice – for often knowing
    the truth but not acting upon it;
forgive me for just going with the crowd.

Lord, we pray for the courts of our and every land –
    that causes and cases be decided in equity and fairness.
You are the eternal judge.
Help me and all who call on you
    to face the heavenly tribunal with confidence,
    assured that your righteousness exceeds all sin.   AMEN.

Readings

Prayer Activity

If you were on trial for being a follower of Jesus, would you be convicted? What is there in your life that would make you innocent or guilty? 'An unexamined life is not worth living' – examine yourself, discover what you are. And, with such knowledge, your own willpower and the grace of God, aim for that conviction – of being a follower of Jesus.

Prayer for the Church

Those involved in Christian counselling and healing

especially the Christian Fellowship of Healing and other similar groups, and any local group in your church or area.

Blessing

Bless me with your peace in Christ now and on the day of judgement.   AMEN.

THE EARLY CHURCH

*Now I appeal to you, brothers and sisters, by the name
of our Lord Jesus Christ, that all of you be in agreement
and that there be no divisions among you, but that you be
united in the same mind and the same purpose.*

~ 1 Corinthians 1:10 ~

Loving God, how long will you put up with us?
You left no written instructions for your Church,
but you did leave us your example.
How have we become so divided?
What are we to make of a Church
of 30,000 denominations world-wide,
each claiming to be your true body?

Nevertheless, what richness in this diversity! –
    different people, different gifts, different opportunities.
Help us to build on our differences,
trusting that your Spirit is at work in us all
and that your message is being carried
    to all the four corners of the world.

Where along the way we have lost the enthusiasm,
the insight, the courage to break new ground
    shown in the life of the young Church,
help us to hear from one another and to hear your Word
so that we recover the Gospel which is new every morning
and feel the presence of Christ with us
as vividly as they did on the first Easter day.

Readings

1 Corinthians 1	*Divisions in the church*
Acts 4:32–7	*Believers share their*
	possessions
1 Corinthians 10:23–11:1	*Do all to the glory of God*
2 Corinthians 4:16–5:10	*Living by faith*

Prayer Activity

> Sit quietly, breathe deeply, let your mind move around
> the area you live and think of all the churches found in
> it. Ask God to breathe his Holy Spirit on each church
> and the people who worship and witness there week
> by week.

Prayer for the Church

As it seeks to develop its spitirual life and become more
aware of the God who is in all things and who is with us in
our daily lives

especially those involved in the Spirituality Initiative.

Blessing

      Bless us, God.
      All of us, God.
      Every one of us.
      Every part of us.
      We want to be full of your love and creativity.
      We want to be full of you.

Ruth Burgess, *A Book of Blessings and How to
Write your Own* (Wild Goose Publications, 2001), p. 148

GENTILES

After greeting them, he [Paul] related one by one the
things that God had done among the Gentiles through
his ministry.

~ Acts 21:19 ~

Love: large enough for all.
Love: broad enough for everyone.
Love: deep enough for the world.
Love: broken for the sinner.
Lover: being born among outsiders.
Love: rising for us all.

Love cannot be contained within any system,
or held exclusive to any one religion.
She cannot be tied down with definitions,
or explained by any one culture.
Love cannot be fenced in by any particular group,
or owned by any denomination.
She cannot be copyrighted by one body,
or held ransom by any particular history.

Love can only be for everyone,
or it cannot be love.
She loves beyond barriers of:
race or language;
sexuality or lifestyle;
culture or heritage;
religion or politics.

God of the Gentiles,
help me welcome love
into my heart, my mind, my decisions;
help me welcome love
into my relationships, my choices, my family;
help me welcome love
into my neighbourhood, my community, my world.
God of the Gentiles,
may I live a love big enough for all.

Readings

Jonah 3:1–10	*A prophet to the Gentiles*
John 4:1–26	*The Samaritan at the well*
Acts 10:9–16	*God's big picnic*
Acts 10:34–43	*Peter's breakthrough*
Romans 9:19–26	*God's anger and mercy*
1 Corinthians 12:12–14	*One Body*
Ephesians 5:1–6	*The Plan*

Prayer Activity

Reflect on the communities that are divided on religious or cultural grounds such as Northern Ireland, or Palestine, or the West and South. Simply be present with these things rather than say things about them. Be present and let the images linger in your mind for a while. Conclude by repeating the first stanza of today's prayer.

Prayer for the Church

Centres to which people may withdraw to renew body and mind and to engage more deeply in worship and study, seeking the relevance of the Gospel for the modern world

especially Scottish Churches' House, Carberry, the Badenoch Christian Centre, the Abbey and MacLeod Centre on Iona, Key House (Falkland) and other retreat centres.

Blessing

May God's grace curve towards you and yours,
may the sky stretch for a thousand acres about you,
may the land forever hold you and give you life,
and may you share this blessing of heaven, always.

MARTYRS

When they heard these things, they became enraged and ground their teeth at Stephen. But filled with the Holy Spirit, he gazed into heaven and saw the glory of God.

~ Acts 7:54–5 ~

'Glorious things of thee are spoken', the ancient hymn declares,
and yet, God, terrible things have been done to those who declared your name.

We wrestle today with the thought of dying for our beliefs,
with the idea of suffering for our faith, being persecuted to death.
For we are of a world that often believes nothing and that at best mocks
or has pity on those with passion and the courage of conviction.

So may we reflect now on those from the Bible who faced rage head on,
who did not back down but kept on proclaiming and who in pain, with death approaching,
remembered Christ, and with faith, in reverence and complete surrender to your cause of love, cried: 'Lord, receive my spirit, do not hold this sin against them'.

As we recall that group of biblical martyrs
who let their lives end for your glory to shine through,
let us learn how to stand strong and make our lives count for Christ in this day.
Let us pray for those who boldly go and suffer the consequences
– who do things we would never do for the gospel.
But above all, let us regain and relive the passion of Christ,
love that is the be-all and end-all,
and glimpses of resurrection that bring life to our dead places,
colour and experience and courage behind our locked doors.

Readings

> Acts 7:44–60   *Stephen's speech and death*
> John 20:19–29   *Resurrection assurance*
> Luke 23:26–43   *Jesus is crucified*

Prayer Activity

Scared? What of? Of whom? Let Jesus receive these fears and anxieties from you, and ask him what he would do.

Prayer for the Church

Those who are in my own congregation, helping it to be part of the living, witnessing Church.

Blessing

> Haven't you heard that Jesus is risen?
> Haven't you heard that Jesus goes on?
> Haven't you heard that Jesus is with us?
> Laughter is living and grieving is gone.

Alison Robertson
from *CH4*, no. 433

TREE OF JESSE/TREE OF LIFE

*A shoot shall come out from the stump of Jesse, and a
branch shall grow out of his roots.*

~ Isaiah 11:1 ~

Rootedness
Trees linking me with the earth beneath my feet
Opening to the depths – history

Standing
Trees conveying my need to be located in space and time
A point of reference – location

Transcendence
Trees expressing my need for expansiveness
Feelings of beyond – ecstasy

Generation upon generation seeing one tree
Wisdom, sacred space, giver of food
where kings were crowned
Justice dispensed

We see our families in trees
Family trees

I am of the tree of Jesse
I am of the tree of life

Wow

My prayer is to live with rootedness that brings life
To stand in a way that upholds truth
To open my life to grow way beyond my hopes and dreams

Readings

Prayer Activity

In Scotland we have the oldest tree in Europe, the yew tree at Fortingall in Perthshire; and there is also the legend that Pontius Pilate was brought up in that area, where his father was posted in the Roman army. Tree of life and tree of death – which holds most meaning for you at this moment?

Prayer for the Church

My own part in the Church and the special gifts I have been given which, in unity with others, build up the body of Christ.

Blessing

As peoples the world over have found blessing in trees
a metaphor for spiritual life, so be it for me here and now.

Earth beneath my feet, root me;
branches of life, stretch me;
trunk of my being, stabilise me.

DAILY BIBLE READINGS

The asterisk* denotes the following Sunday's readings and psalm prescribed in the Revised Common Lectionary (and as in Common Order*), and the readings set for special festivals.*

These readings come from the Australian publication, *With Love to the World*, a daily Bible-reading guide prepared in the Uniting Church in Australia and used throughout Australia and increasingly world-wide. It contains short notes on each passage by writers who are knowledgeable about the Biblical background, as well as other material. It is published quarterly. Copies can be ordered through the Church of Scotland's Office for Worship. The likely annual subscription would be £10.00.

NOVEMBER 2005

Mon	21	1 Corinthians 1:1–3
Tue	22	1 Corinthians 1:4–9 (3–9*)
Wed	23	Mark 13:24–31
Thu	24	Mark 13:32–7 (24–37*)
Fri	25	Isaiah 63:15–19
Sat	26	Isaiah 64:1–9*
Sun	27	Psalm 80:1–7, 17–19*
		First Sunday of Advent

Mon	28	2 Peter 3:1–7
Tue	29	2 Peter 3:8–15a*
Wed	30	2 Peter 3:15b–18

DECEMBER

Thu	1	Mark 1:1–8*
Fri	2	Isaiah 40:1–5
Sat	3	Isaiah 40:6–11 (1–11)*
Sun	4	Psalm 85:1–2, 8–13*

Mon	5	1 Thessalonians 5:12–15
Tue	6	1 Thessalonians 5:16–28 (16–24*)
Wed	7	John 1:6–8, 19–28*
Thu	8	John 3:23–30

Fri	9	Isaiah 61:1–11 (1–4, 8–11*)
Sat	10	Psalm 126*
Sun	11	Luke 1:47–55*

Mon	12	Romans 16:1–16
Tue	13	Romans 16:17–24
Wed	14	Romans 16:25–7*
Thu	15	Luke 1:26–38*
Fri	16	2 Samuel 7:1–11 (1–11, 16*)
Sat	17	2 Samuel 7:12–17
Sun	18	Psalm 89:1–4, 19–26*

Mon	19	Isaiah 62:1–5
Tue	20	Isaiah 62:6–12*
Wed	21	Psalm 97*
Thu	22	Titus 3:4–7*
Fri	23	Luke 1:57–66
Sat	24	Luke 2:1–7
Sun	25	Luke 2:(1–7,) 8–20*

Mon	26	Genesis 15:1–6, 21:1–3
Tue	27	Isaiah 61:10–62:3*
Wed	28	Psalm 148*
Thu	29	Galatians 4:4–7*
Fri	30	Numbers 6:22–7*
Sat	31	Luke 2:15–21

JANUARY 2006

Sun	1	Luke 2:22–40*

Mon	2	Exodus 14:15–22
Tue	3	Acts 11:4–18
Wed	4	Acts 19:1–7*
Thu	5	Mark 1:4–11*
Fri	6	Ephesians 3:1–12
		Epiphany of the Lord
Sat	7	Genesis 1:1–5*
Sun	8	Psalm 29*

Mon	9	1 Corinthians 6:1–11
Tue	10	1 Corinthians 6:12–20*
Wed	11	John 1:43–51*
Thu	12	Psalm 63:1–8
Fri	13	1 Samuel 3:1–10*
Sat	14	1 Samuel 3:11–20
Sun	15	Psalm 139:1–6, 13–18*
Mon	16	1 Corinthians 7:17–24
Tue	17	1 Corinthians 7:25–31 (29–31*)
Wed	18	1 Corinthians 7:32–40
Thu	19	Mark 1:14–20*
Fri	20	Jonah 1:1–17
Sat	21	Jonah 3:1–10 (1–5, 10*)
Sun	22	Psalm 62:5–12*
Mon	23	1 Corinthians 8:1–6
Tue	24	1 Corinthians 8:7–13 (1–13*)
Wed	25	Mark 1:21–8*
Thu	26	Deuteronomy 6:10–18
Fri	27	Deuteronomy 18:9–14
Sat	28	Deuteronomy 18:15–22 (15–20*)
Sun	29	Psalm 111*
Mon	30	1 Corinthians 9:1–15
Tue	31	1 Corinthians 9:16–23*

FEBRUARY

Wed	1	2 Kings 4:18–21, 32–7
Thu	2	Mark 1:29–39*
Fri	3	Job 7:1–7
Sat	4	Isaiah 40:21–31*
Sun	5	Psalm 147 (1–11, 20c*)
Mon	6	1 Corinthians 9:24–7*
Tue	7	Leviticus 13:1–2, 45–6
Wed	8	Psalm 32
Thu	9	Mark 1:40–5*

Fri	10	2 Kings 5:1–14*
Sat	11	2 Kings 5:15–19a
Sun	12	Psalm 30*

Mon	13	2 Kings 5:19b–27
Tue	14	2 Corinthians 1:3–14
Wed	15	2 Corinthians 1:15–24 (18–22*)
Thu	16	Mark 2:1–12*
Fri	17	Isaiah 43:8–13
Sat	18	Isaiah 43:18–25*
Sun	19	Psalm 41*

Mon	20	Mark 2:13–22
Tue	21	2 Corinthians 3:1–6
Wed	22	2 Corinthians 4:3–6*
Thu	23	Exodus 34:29–35
Fri	24	Mark 9:2–9*
Sat	25	2 Kings 2:1–12*
Sun	26	Psalm 50:1–6*

| Mon | 27 | 2 Corinthians 5:11–15 |
| Tue | 28 | 2 Corinthians 5:20b–6:10 |

MARCH

Wed	1	Matthew 6:1–6, 16–21
		Ash Wednesday
Thu	2	Mark 1:9–15*
Fri	3	1 Peter 3:18–22*
Sat	4	Genesis 9:8–17*
Sun	5	Psalm 25:1–10*

Mon	6	Psalm 105:1–11
Tue	7	Romans 4:13–25*
Wed	8	Mark 8:31–8*
Thu	9	Mark 10:32–4, 42b–45
Fri	10	Genesis 17:1–16 (1–7, 15–16*)
Sat	11	Genesis 22:1–18
Sun	12	Psalm 22:23–31*

Mon	13	1 Corinthians 1:18–25*
Tue	14	Mark 11:12–25
Wed	15	John 2:13–22*
Thu	16	Exodus 20:1–17*
Fri	17	Deuteronomy 30:11–20
Sat	18	Romans 7:13–25
Sun	19	Psalm 19*

Mon	20	2 Chronicles 36:14–23
Tue	21	Psalm 137:1–6
Wed	22	Ephesians 2:1–10*
Thu	23	Ephesians 2:11–22
Fri	24	John 3:14–21*
Sat	25	Numbers 21:4–9*
Sun	26	Psalm 107:1–3, 17–22*

Mon	27	Hebrews 5:5–10*
Tue	28	John 12:12–19
Wed	29	John 12:20–33*
Thu	30	Deuteronomy 30:1–3, 6–10
Fri	31	Psalm 119:9–16*

APRIL

| Sat | 1 | Jeremiah 31:31–4* |
| Sun | 2 | Psalm 51:1–12* |

Mon	3	Mark 11:1–11
Tue	4	Psalm 31:9–16*
Wed	5	Mark 14:26–52
Thu	6	Mark 14:53–72
Fri	7	Mark 15:1–15
Sat	8	Mark 15:16–24
Sun	9	Mark 15:25–39 (14:1–15:47*)
		Psalm/Passion Sunday

| Mon | 10 | Isaiah 25:6–9* |
| Tue | 11 | Acts 10:34–43* |

Wed	12	Psalm 118:1–2, 14–24*
Thu	13	Mark 14:12–26
Fri	14	Hebrews 4:14–16, 5:7–9
		Good Friday
Sat	15	1 Corinthians 15:1–11*
Sun	16	Mark 16:1–8*
		Easter Day

Mon	17	John 20:1–8
Tue	18	John 20:19–31*
Wed	19	Psalm 148
Thu	20	Isaiah 26:2–9, 19
Fri	21	1 John 1:1–2:2*
Sat	22	Acts 4:32–5*
Sun	23	Psalm 133*

Mon	24	Micah 4:1–5
Tue	25	John 15:9–17
Wed	26	1 John 2:18–29
Thu	27	1 John 3:1–7*
Fri	28	Luke 24:35–48 (36b–48*)
Sat	29	Acts 3:12–19*
Sun	30	Psalm 4*

MAY

Mon	1	1 John 3:16–24*
Tue	2	1 John 4:1–6
Wed	3	John 10:11–18*
Thu	4	Ezekiel 34:1–10
Fri	5	Acts 4:5–12*
Sat	6	Acts 4:23–33
Sun	7	Psalm 23*

Mon	8	1 John 4:7–21*
Tue	9	John 14:15–21
Wed	10	John 15:1–8*
Thu	11	Deuteronomy 4:32–40

Fri	12	Acts 8:26–40*
Sat	13	Acts 9:26–31
Sun	14	Psalm 22:25–31*

Mon	15	1 John 5:1–6*
Tue	16	John 15:9–17*
Wed	17	John 15:18–6:4a
Thu	18	Isaiah 45:11–19
Fri	19	Acts 10:44–8*
Sat	20	Acts 11:19–30
Sun	21	Psalm 98*

Mon	22	John 17:6–12
Tue	23	John 17:13–19 (6–19*)
Wed	24	1 John 5:9–13*
Thu	25	Psalm 93
		Ascension of the Lord
Fri	26	Exodus 28:1–30
Sat	27	Acts 1:15–26 (15–17, 21–6*)
Sun	28	Psalm 1*

Mon	29	John 15:26–16:4
Tue	30	John 16:5–15 (15:26–7, 16:4b–15*)
Wed	31	Romans 8:22–7*

JUNE

Thu	1	Acts 2:1–13
Fri	2	Acts 2:14–21 (1–21*)
Sat	3	Ezekiel 37:1–14*
Sun	4	Psalm 104:24–34, 35b*
		Pentecost

Mon	5	Psalm 33:13–21
Tue	6	John 3:1–17*
Wed	7	John 5:16–23
Thu	8	Romans 8:12–17*
Fri	9	Deuteronomy 4:32–40
Sat	10	Isaiah 6:1–8*
Sun	11	Psalm 29*

Mon	12	2 Corinthians 4:13–5:1
Tue	13	2 Corinthians 5:6–10, (11–13,) 14–17*
Wed	14	Mark 4:26–34*
Thu	15	1 Samuel 3:1–10 (11–20)
Fri	16	1 Samuel 8:4–11, (12–15,) 16–20 (11:14–15)
Sat	17	1 Samuel 15:34–16:13*
Sun	18	Psalm 20*

Mon	19	1 Samuel 17:(1a, 4–11, 19–23,) 32–49*
Tue	20	1 Samuel 17:32–51
Wed	21	1 Samuel 17:57–18:16
Thu	22	2 Corinthians 5:18–21
Fri	23	2 Corinthians 6:1–13*
Sat	24	Mark 4:35–41*
Sun	25	Psalm 9:9–20*

Mon	26	2 Corinthians 7:2–4, 8–16
Tue	27	2 Corinthians 8:7–15*
Wed	28	2 Corinthians 9:6–15
Thu	29	Mark 5:21–43*
Fri	30	2 Samuel 19:8–17

JULY

| Sat | 1 | 2 Samuel 1:1, 17–27* |
| Sun | 2 | Psalm 130* |

Mon	3	2 Samuel 5:1–16 (1–5, 9–10*)
Tue	4	2 Corinthians 11:1–15
Wed	5	2 Corinthians 11:16–33
Thu	6	2 Corinthians 12:2–10*
Fri	7	Mark 6:1–6a
Sat	8	Mark 6:6b–13 (1–13*)
Sun	9	Psalm 48*

| Mon | 10 | 2 Corinthians 13:1–14 |
| Tue | 11 | Mark 6:14–29* |

Wed	12	Psalm 26
Thu	13	2 Samuel 6:1–15 (1–5, 12b–19*)
Fri	14	2 Samuel 6:16–23
Sat	15	Mark 6:14–29*
Sun	16	Psalm 24*
Mon	17	Ephesians 1:15–23
Tue	18	Ephesians 2:1–10
Wed	19	Ephesians 2:11–22*
Thu	20	Mark 6:30–44 (30–4, 53–6*)
Fri	21	Mark 6:45–56
Sat	22	2 Samuel 7:1–17 (1–14a*)
Sun	23	Psalm 89:20–37*
Mon	24	John 6:1–15 (1–21*)
Tue	25	John 6:16–21
Wed	26	Ephesians 3:1–13
Thu	27	Ephesians 3:14–21*
Fri	28	2 Samuel 9:1–13
Sat	29	2 Samuel 11:1–17 (1–15*)
Sun	30	Psalm 14*
Mon	31	2 Samuel 11:18–26

AUGUST

Tue	1	2 Samuel 12:1–15a (11:26–12:13a*)
Wed	2	Ephesians 4:1–16*
Thu	3	Ephesians 4:17–24
Fri	4	John 6:22–7 (24–35*)
Sat	5	John 6:28–35
Sun	6	Psalm 51:1–12*
Mon	7	John 6:35–40 (35, 41–51*)
Tue	8	John 6:41–51
Wed	9	2 Samuel 13:1–2, 6–15, 20–2, 27b–39
Thu	10	2 Samuel 15:1–18, 30

Fri	11	2 Samuel 18:5–9, 15, 31–3; 19:5–8 (18:5–9, 15, 31–3*)
Sat	12	Ephesians 4:25–5:2*
Sun	13	Psalm 130*

Mon	14	Ephesians 5:3–14
Tue	15	Ephesians 5:15–20*
Wed	16	Ephesians 5:21–33
Thu	17	John 6:51–8*
Fri	18	1 Kings 1:1–4, 15–21, 32–40, 47–53
Sat	19	1 Kings 2:1–12, 3:3–14 (2:10–12, 3:3–14*)
Sun	20	Psalm 111*

Mon	21	John 6:56–71 (56–69*)
Tue	22	Ephesians 6:10–17 (10–20*)
Wed	23	Ephesians 6:18–24
Thu	24	1 Kings 5:2, 5–6; 5:10–6:1, 7, 11–22
Fri	25	1 Kings 6:23–37
Sat	26	1 Kings 8:(1–6, 10–11,) 22–30, 41–3*
Sun	27	Psalm 84*

Mon	28	James 1:1–11 (17–27*)
Tue	29	James 1:12–18
Wed	30	James 1:19–27
Thu	31	Mark 7:1–13 (1–8, 14–15, 21–3*)

SEPTEMBER

Fri	1	Mark 7:14–23
Sat	2	Song of Solomon 2:8–13*
Sun	3	Psalm 45:1–2, 6–9*

Mon	4	Proverbs 22:1–10 (1–2, 8–9, 22–3*)
Tue	5	Proverbs 22:17–25
Wed	6	James 2:1–13 [1–10, (11–13,) 14–17*]

Thu	7	James 2:14–26
Fri	8	Mark 7:24–30 (24–37*)
Sat	9	Mark 7:31–7
Sun	10	Psalm 125*

Mon	11	Mark 8:1–10
Tue	12	Mark 8:11–21
Wed	13	Mark 8:22–6
Thu	14	Mark 8:27–38*
Fri	15	James 3:1–12*
Sat	16	Proverbs 1:1–7, 20–3, 32–3 (20–33*)
Sun	17	Psalm 19*

Mon	18	Mark 9:30–7*
Tue	19	James 3:13–18 (3:13–4:3, 7–8a*)
Wed	20	James 4:1–7
Thu	21	James 4:8–17
Fri	22	James 5:1–12
Sat	23	Proverbs 31:10–31*
Sun	24	Psalm 1*

Mon	25	James 5:13–20*
Tue	26	Mark 9:38–50*
Wed	27	Esther 1:1–21 (7:1–6, 9–10, 9:20–2*)
Thu	28	Esther 2:1–11, 15–23
Fri	29	Esther 3:1–11
Sat	30	Esther 4:1–17

OCTOBER

Sun	1	Psalm 124*

Mon	2	Esther 5:1–4, 7:1–10
Tue	3	Esther 8:1–12, 15–17
Wed	4	Esther 9:1–2, 16–28
Thu	5	Mark 10:1–16 (2–16*)
Fri	6	Hebrews 1:1–4, 2:5–12*
Sat	7	Job 1:1, 2:1–10*
Sun	8	Psalm 26*

Mon	9	Mark 10:17–27 (17–31*)
Tue	10	Mark 10:28–34
Wed	11	Hebrews 3:1–15
Thu	12	Hebrews 3:16–4:11
Fri	13	Hebrews 4:12–16*
Sat	14	Job 23:1–9, 16–17*
Sun	15	Psalm 22:1–15*

Mon	16	Mark 10:35–45*
Tue	17	Hebrews 5:1–10*
Wed	18	Hebrews 5:11–6:8
Thu	19	Hebrews 6:9–12
Fri	20	Job 38:1–7 (1–7, 34–41*)
Sat	21	Job 38:34–41
Sun	22	Psalm 104:1–9, 24, 35c*

Mon	23	Hebrews 6:13–20
Tue	24	Hebrews 7:11–22
Wed	25	Hebrews 7:23–8*
Thu	26	Hebrews 8:1–13
Fri	27	Job 42:1–6, 10–17*
Sat	28	Mark 10:46–52*
Sun	29	Psalm 34:1–8 (19–22*)

Mon	30	Romans 5:1–11
Tue	31	1 Peter 2:1–10

NOVEMBER

Wed	1	Revelations 21:1–7*
Thu	2	Hebrews 9:11–14*
Fri	3	Mark 12:28–34*
Sat	4	Ruth 1:1–22 (1–18*)
Sun	5	Psalm 146*

Mon	6	Mark 12:38–44*
Tue	7	Hebrews 9:24–8*
Wed	8	Hebrews 10:1–10
Thu	9	Ruth 2:1–12, 17–23

Fri	10	Ruth 3:1–18 (3:1–5, 4:13–17*)
Sat	11	Ruth 4:1–6, 9–17
Sun	12	Psalm 127*
Mon	13	Mark 13:1–8*
Tue	14	Mark 13:9–13
Wed	15	Hebrews 10:1–10
Thu	16	Hebrews 10:11–25*
Fri	17	Hebrews 10:26–31
Sat	18	1 Samuel 1:4–20*
Sun	19	1 Samuel 2:1–10*
Mon	20	John 18:33–7*
Tue	21	Revelation 1:4b–8*
Wed	22	Daniel 7:1, 9–14
Thu	23	Psalm 93
Fri	24	2 Samuel 22:1–16
Sat	25	2 Samuel 23:1–7*
Sun	26	Psalm 132:1–12 (13–18*)
		Christ the King

SERVING OVERSEAS WITH THE CHURCH OF SCOTLAND

with their families

(to be added to the Prayer for the Church for each day)

Day 1   MALAWI: Andy and Felicity Gaston with Katy and Daniel

Day 2   MALAWI: Helen Scott

Day 3   ZAMBIA: Colin Johnston, Georgina and Brian Payne

Day 4   KENYA: Elaine McKinnon, Alison Wilkinson

Day 5   SOUTH AFRICA: Graham and Sandra Duncan

Day 6   NEPAL: Marianne Karsgaard, Christine Stone

Day 7   BRUSSELS: Matthew Ross

Day 8   TRINIDAD: Garwell (John) and Claudette Bacchas with Kerri-Ann

Day 9   CENTRAL ASIA: Alastair and Mary Morrice

Day 10   ISRAEL AND PALESTINE: Jeneffer Zielinski, Malti Joshi

Day 11   BANGLADESH: David and Sarah Hall with Rebecca

Day 12   ISRAEL AND PALESTINE: Clarence and Joan Musgrave

Day 13   ISRAEL AND PALESTINE: Karen Anderson

Day 14   ISRAEL AND PALESTINE: Gwen and Mark Thompson

Day 15   JAMAICA: Margaret Fowler

Day 16   SRI LANKA: John and Patricia Purves

Day 17   BERMUDA: Alan and Elizabeth Garrity

ACKNOWLEDGEMENTS

Scriptural quotations, unless otherwise stated, are from the *New Revised Standard Version*, © 1989 Division of Christian Education of the National Council of the Churches of Christ in the United States of America, published by Oxford University Press.

The blessings at the conclusion of each day, whose sources are given, are reproduced by permission.

The list of Daily Bible Readings is from *With Love to the World* and is reproduced by kind permission.

Pray Now 2006 was prepared by members of the Panel on Worship's Prayer and Devotion Committee: Gayle Taylor, Roddy Hamilton, Douglas Lamb, Lyn Peden, Jenny Williams, Jim Campbell and Douglas Galbraith.

For further information about *Pray Now* and other publications from the Office for Worship and Doctrine, contact:

>Office for Worship and Doctrine
>Church of Scotland
>121 George Street
>Edinburgh EH2 4YN
>Tel: 0131-225 5722 ext. 359
>Fax: 0131-220 3113
>e-mail: wordoc@cofscotland.org.uk

We gratefully acknowledge the following for their kind permission to reproduce the pictures used in this book:

Torvald Lekvam (torvald), 'Disco 16', on pp. 36–7 and on the cover.

Neza Cerin, 'Umbrella 2', on p. 31; and 'Colours 2', on p. 25.

Gabor Palla, 'Mosaic', on p. 45.